W9-ATD-685

Our Values

MAKING GOOD CHOICES

By Steffi Cavell-Clarke

Crabtree Publishing Company
www.crabtreebooks.com
1-800-387-7650

Published in Canada
Crabtree Publishing
616 Welland Avenue
St. Catharines, ON
L2M 5V6

Published in the United States
Crabtree Publishing
PMB 59051
350 Fifth Ave, 59th Floor
New York, NY 10118

Published by Crabtree Publishing Company in 2017

First Published by Book Life in 2016
Copyright © 2017 Book Life

Author
Steffi Cavell-Clarke

Editors
Grace Jones
Janine Deschenes

Design
Natalie Carr

Proofreader
Crystal Sikkens

**Production coordinator and
prepress technician (interior)**
Margaret Amy Salter

Prepress technician (covers)
Ken Wright

Print coordinator
Katherine Berti

Photographs
All images by Shutterstock

Printed in Hong Kong/012017/BK20161024

Library and Archives Canada Cataloguing in Publication

Cavell-Clarke, Steffi, author
    Making good choices / Steffi Cavell-Clarke.

(Our values)
Issued in print and electronic formats.
ISBN 978-0-7787-3262-4 (hardback).--ISBN 978-0-7787-3328-7
(paperback).--ISBN 978-1-4271-1893-6 (html)

    1. Decision making--Moral and ethical aspects--Juvenile literature.
I. Title.

BJ1419.C38 2016   j179'.9   C2016-906682-7
                                        C2016-906683-5

Library of Congress Cataloging-in-Publication Data

CIP available at Library of Congress

CONTENTS

Words that are bolded, like **this**, can be found in the glossary on page 24.

WHAT ARE VALUES?

Values are the things that you believe are important, such as working hard at school. The ways we think and behave depend on our values. Values teach us how we should **respect** each other and ourselves. Sharing the same values as others helps us work and live together in a **community**.

Respecting others

Making good choices

Understanding different beliefs

Values make our communities better places to live. Think about the values in your community. What is important to you and the people around you?

Telling the truth

Working together

Listening to others

5

MAKING A CHOICE

Making good choices is an important value. We all have to make choices. We make a choice every time we decide what to eat or what to wear. These choices can be simple. Other choices are more difficult to make, such as how to solve a problem. The choices we make can change our actions and affect the people around us.

A lot of things can **influence** our choices. We can make choices based on what we like or dislike, as well as what we think is right or wrong. When we make a choice based on what we think is right or wrong, we are following our values.

WHY ARE CHOICES IMPORTANT?

Making our own choices is an important part of our **freedom**. When making a choice, it is important to think of how it might affect others. We should always make choices that show our respect for others, and choose to do things that make ourselves and the people around us happy.

Being able to make choices means that we are free to decide how we live our lives. We can choose what we wear, what we eat, and how we treat others.

I want to be a teacher.

I want to be a doctor.

I want to be an artist.

It's important to choose goals for the future, such as what you'd like to be when you grow up. To reach your goals, you have to make good choices—such as doing your homework or working hard in class.

MAKING THE RIGHT CHOICES

Our choices can affect the people around us, so it is important that we think carefully about the **outcomes** of our choices before we make them.

To help us make the right choice, we must remember to treat others the way that we would like to be treated.

Sometimes it can be difficult to make a choice because we are worried it will have a **negative** outcome, or we are afraid others won't agree with our choice. It's important that you choose to do what you feel is right. You can also ask friends and family members that you trust to help you make the right choices.

CHANGING OUR CHOICES

It can be difficult to think of all the outcomes of our choices before we make them. Sometimes, we make choices that have negative outcomes. When we do this, it is important to change our choices to make things better.

Kelly learned about **pollution** at school. She learned that her choice to get to school by car adds to the air pollution in her community. She decided to walk to school with her mom instead. She knew that her new choice would help look after the **environment**.

BEING RESPONSIBLE

When you make **responsible** choices, you can build strong relationships with others because you become someone they can trust. You can make responsible choices by thinking about how your choices affect others. Think about others' feelings and choose to help them when you can.

You can show that you are responsible and trustworthy by following through on what you say you are going to do. Kavita promised her little sister that she would help her tie her shoelaces. She helps her every morning before going to school. Kavita's choice to help her sister shows she is responsible and thinks about others.

LISTENING TO OTHERS

When you are making choices, it can be important to listen to other people. Listening to others' thoughts and feelings can help you think about how your choices may affect them. You can also ask others' for help when making choices.

Sometimes our friends can influence our choices. We may feel **pressured** into doing something that we did not choose to do ourselves. It can be hard to say no to a friend, but we always have a choice and sometimes it is important to say no.

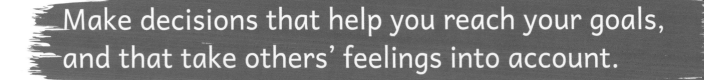

Make decisions that help you reach your goals, and that take others' feelings into account.

17

MAKING CHOICES AT SCHOOL

At school, you have rules to follow and classmates to think about. It is important to make the choice to listen, learn, and behave at school. Learning about new things can help us understand what is right and wrong.

At school, you should think about how your choices affect your classmates. Make choices that show your classmates that they can count on you.

If you are part of a group project or school sports team, choose to do your best and finish your part.

MAKING CHOICES AT HOME

Be responsible at home by doing the things you say you are going to do, such as helping to wash the dishes. Choosing to be thoughtful and kind to the people we live with is very important. Show others you respect and care about them by making choices that have good outcomes.

The choices we make at home affect the way we feel. Rory chooses to play soccer with his friends after school to have fun and get some exercise. Making good choices at home helps us feel happy and build strong relationships with family and friends.

MAKING A DIFFERENCE

Do you have any old toys or clothes that you don't use anymore? If so, you can choose to **donate** these to a **charity**. This means that someone who doesn't have a lot of money can still get the things they need.

DONATE!

If you notice a classmate at school who is being left out or seems upset, you can choose to ask them how they are. You can also ask them to join in a game to cheer them up. Choose to do what you know is right, even if others don't agree.

By making good choices, you can make a difference for many people!

GLOSSARY

charity [CHAR-i-tee] An organization that helps those in need
community [kuh-MYOO-ni-tee] A group of people who live, work, and play in a place
donate [DOH-neyt] To make a free gift or contribution toward a cause
environment [en-VAHY-ruh n muh nt] Your surroundings
freedom [FREE-duh m] Being allowed to do something
influence [IN-floo-uh-ns] To be able to change something
law [law] Rules made by government that a community has to follow
negative [neg-uh-tiv] Without positive qualities
outcomes [OUT-kuhms] The results of an action or process
pollution [puh-LOO-shuh n] Something that is harmful to the environment
pressured [PRESH-er-ed] Trying to force someone to do something
respect [ri-SPEKT] The act of giving something or someone the attention it deserves
responsible [ri-spon-suh-buhl] Reliable or dependable

INDEX